I Remember My Breath

Mindful Breathing for All My Feelings

Lynn Rummel
illustrated by Karen Bunting

free spirit
PUBLISHING®

Library of Congress Cataloging-in-Publication Data
Names: Rummel, Lynn, author. | Bunting, Karen (Illustrator), illustrator.
Title: I remember my breath : mindful breathing for all my feelings / LynnRummel ; illustrated by Karen Bunting.
Description: Huntington Beach : Free Spirit Publishing, an imprint of Teacher Created Materials, Inc., [2023] | Audience: Ages 4–8 | Audience: Grades 2–3
Identifiers: LCCN 2022020574 (print) | LCCN 2022020575 (ebook) | ISBN 9781631985713 (hardback) | ISBN 9781631985737 (ebook)
Subjects: LCSH: Respiration—Juvenile literature. | Breathing exercises—Juvenile literature. | Mindfulness (Psychology)—Juvenile literature.
Classification: LCC RA782 .R78 2023 (print) | LCC RA782 (ebook) | DDC 613/.192—dc23/eng/20220628
LC record available at https://lccn.loc.gov/2022020574
LC ebook record available at https://lccn.loc.gov/2022020575

Edited by Christine Zuchora-Walske
Cover and interior design by Emily Dyer and Colleen Pidel
Illustrated by Karen Bunting

Printed in China

Free Spirit Publishing
An imprint of Teacher Created Materials
9850 51st Avenue, Suite 100
Minneapolis, MN 55442
(612) 338-2068
help4kids@freespirit.com
freespirit.com

For Kenny, Molly, and Nicholas.

I have so many feelings.
Sometimes it's hard to know
what to do with them.

Paying attention to my breath can help.

My breath is always with me.

My breath helps me know what to do.

I feel **worried**.

The what-ifs are rising,
growing,
pretending they are real.

I remember my breath.
My breath is the wind.

It blows steady and strong.
It blows the what-ifs
away . . . away . . . away . . .
until they are so small I can't see them anymore.

I feel **EXCITED**.

I smile on the outside
and on the inside.
I feel a warm glow spread out
from my heart in all directions.

I remember my breath.
My breath is a paintbrush.

It brightens the colors,
captures the memories,
carries the joy of this moment
right back into my heart.

I feel **sad**.

A heavy feeling
weighs me down . . .
down . . . down.

I remember my breath.
My breath is an umbrella.

As I breathe in and out,
the umbrella opens and rises and stretches.
It catches and holds the weight.
Right now I am here. Right now I am safe.

I feel **nervous**.

Butterflies flutter wildly in my belly and my chest.

I remember my breath.
My breath is a net.

It swoops down and up, left and right.
I breathe in and catch butterflies.
I breathe out and let them go.
They fly free.

Words come fast and hot from my mouth.
They burn my face.

I remember my breath.

My breath is rushing water.

It's clear and cold.
It puts out the fire inside me.
It cools my face.
It washes my hot words away.

I feel **embarrassed**.

Laughter pounds in my ears
like a hundred beating drums.

I remember my breath.
My breath is snow.

It falls on the drums,
blankets them, hushes them.
Shhh . . . shhh . . . shhh . . .
I find my smile. I find peace.

I feel so many feelings.

I remember my breath.

My breath is always with me.

I breathe in, and I breathe out.
I can handle all my feelings when
I remember my breath.

Mindfulness and Mindful Breathing: A Guide for Caring Adults

You Chose This Book for a Beloved Child

The little people in our lives can sometimes be overwhelmed by big emotions. When this happens, it is our job to share with them what we have learned about experiencing and coping with a variety of feelings. Mindfulness is one important tool for understanding and managing emotions. This book offers a simple introduction to mindfulness through rhythm, imagery, and affirming messages for young children and their families. Thank you for sharing it with the children in your life.

What Is Mindfulness?

Mindfulness is the human state of being fully present. People of all ages may find it difficult to be in this state. We struggle with all the distractions and stressful thoughts we experience throughout each day. But the more we practice mindfulness, the easier it becomes.

Mindfulness practice can take many forms. For children, awareness of breath is a helpful and easy-to-learn form. You could introduce children to mindfulness practice by inviting them to lie on their backs, place a stuffed animal on their bellies, and watch the animals move up and down on their bellies as they breathe.

The benefits of mindfulness are many. Scientific evidence suggests that regular mindfulness practice can relieve stress, reduce the risk of heart disease, lower blood pressure, reduce chronic pain, improve quality of sleep, and even calm some digestive discomforts. For children, perhaps the greatest benefit of practicing mindfulness is in emotional regulation.

I Remember My Breath was born from a conversation I had with my son on our way to preschool when he was four. As we neared the school parking lot, I heard his quivering voice from the back seat: "Mom, I have dose butta-fwies in my tummy again." He was often nervous about going to school, and this time he was experiencing a secondary fear of the "butterflies" too. As adults, we know this feeling as anxiety. My four-year-old just knew it felt like butterflies. He didn't like it, and he didn't know what to do about it.

I invited him to imagine his breath was a net. I suggested that he could breathe in to catch the butterflies in his tummy and breathe out to release them into the air. This simple mindful breathing gave him the power he needed to get through that moment—and many others in the years to come.

Mindfulness and Feelings

As you read this book with children and explore the emotions it describes, I hope it will spark conversations about times when you have felt these feelings. The characters in *I Remember My Breath* experience worry, excitement, happiness, sadness, nervousness, anger, and embarrassment. Children may experience many other emotions too but might not yet have names for them: anxiety, guilt, jealousy, irritation, edginess, awkwardness, reluctance . . . the list goes on and on.

Most children know the names of three emotions: sad, happy, and angry (or mad). But there are more! It is important for children to learn to name those other emotions too, and to recognize how they feel physically and what thoughts they bring.

It is essential for all people—young, old, and in-between—to be aware of our own thoughts and feelings and to know that we can experience our emotions safely and manage our physical and mental responses to them. One key way we can do this is by mindful breathing, or bringing attention to our breath. Our breath is always

with us, so it is the foundation of mindfulness and emotional self-regulation.

This book addresses each emotion in three steps: (1) name the feeling, (2) sit with it—notice without judgment how this feeling affects your thoughts and your body, and (3) bring your attention to your breath. The book uses imagery and rhythm to show children identifying and coping with a variety of emotions through mindfulness and awareness of breath.

For example, when the girl experiences anger, she doesn't rush to get rid of the feeling. Rather, she names it ("I feel angry") and notices her thoughts and physical feelings. ("Words come fast and hot from my mouth. They burn my face.") Then she turns her attention to her breath ("I remember my breath") and compares it to rushing water, which helps her self-soothe and self-regulate this strong emotion.

Activities

All feelings are okay—even the uncomfortable ones. It's what we do with them that matters. Following are some simple activities you can do with children individually or in small groups to help them recognize and understand emotions, talk about their feelings, and decide what to do with them.

Belly Breathing

Invite children to choose one small stuffed animal each. Choose one for yourself too. Lie on your backs and place your stuffed animals on your bellies, just below your ribs. Guide children to join you in breathing in and out, in and out . . . watching the stuffed animals rise and fall. For younger children, you might suggest they imagine they are gently rocking the animals to sleep with the rhythm of their breath. During this activity, kindly remind children to stay silent and to focus only on the rise and fall of the stuffed animals.

Feelings Charades

Take turns acting out feelings. Invite each actor to show an emotion through facial expressions and body language. The audience can use these clues to guess how the actor feels. After each turn, discuss together how that emotion feels physically to you. Does your heart beat faster? Do you feel heavy on your feet? Do you get tingles of excitement in your fingertips? Then talk about times when you have felt this way in the past.

Face Collage

If you're doing this activity with an individual child, you'll need a big sheet of paper or posterboard. If you're working with a group of children, a large roll of craft paper or butcher paper would be ideal. Brainstorm a list of emotions with children. Divide the paper into enough sections for all the emotions listed. Label each section with one of those emotions. Invite children to cut out pictures of faces from old magazines, newspapers, and catalogs; sort the faces according to the feelings they show; and glue them to the corresponding section of the paper to create a face collage.

Freeze Frames

Discuss with children some real-life scenarios in which they have felt various emotions. For example, you might start by asking, "Can you think of a time when you felt embarrassed?" Invite them to act out these scenarios (taking turns if you're in a group setting). Call out "Freeze!" when a decision about an action comes up. Talk about the choices the person has and what could result from each. If a scene demonstrates embarrassment, freeze the actor at a point when they realize something embarrassing has happened. Discuss the actor's options. They could run, yell, cry, laugh, start over, or do something else in this situation. What might result from each choice?

About the Author and Illustrator

Lynn Rummel is a licensed speech-language pathologist and certified professional school counselor. While working as an elementary school counselor for nine years, she taught mindfulness and breath awareness strategies to many of her students. Currently, Lynn operates a pediatric speech and language therapy private practice in South Florida, where she lives with her husband, two children, and pug. She specializes in articulation, literacy, and social and emotional skills. Children's picture books are among her favorite therapy materials for all ages.

Karen Bunting is an illustrator currently based in Bristol, UK. She lives with her partner and two cheeky cats, she loves to travel, and she has also lived in Tokyo and Seville. Karen enjoys expressing the quirky side of life in her illustrations, inspired by vintage children's books.